Growing Up

First published 2023 by Nosy Crow Ltd.
Wheat Wharf, 27a Shad Thames
London, SE1 2XZ, UK

This edition published 2024 by Nosy Crow Inc.
145 Lincoln Road
Lincoln, MA 01773, USA

www.nosycrow.us

ISBN 979-8-88777-078-9

Nosy Crow and associated logos are trademarks
and/or registered trademarks of Nosy Crow Ltd.

Used under license.

Text by Rachel Greener
Text © Nosy Crow 2023
Illustrations © Clare Owen 2023

Library of Congress Catalog Card Number Pending.

Printed in China following rigorous ethical sourcing standards.

Papers used by Nosy Crow are made from wood
grown in sustainable forests.

1 3 5 7 9 10 8 6 4 2

Growing Up

written by
Rachel Greener

illustrated by
Clare Owen

You were a baby once. Now you are a child. It may be hard to imagine, but every single adult who has ever lived was once a child, just like you.

Think about all the things that have changed since you were a baby. For a start, you are probably much bigger, and you might look really different!

Your brain has been growing too! Your brain controls your body and does all your thinking. It has been learning lots and lots about the world and how to live in it.

Every day, all of us grow a tiny bit older, and every day, often without knowing it, our bodies are changing in one way or another.

Some of the changes you go through as you get older will have happened to every single adult you know!

So how do you get from being a child to being a grown-up?

When most babies are born, they are usually called boys or girls based on what their bodies look like. This is called the baby's biological sex.

Babies born with a penis and testicles are called boys or males. The penis is used to pee.

Babies born with a vulva are called girls or females. Babies born with a vulva usually have a womb and two ovaries inside their body.

A tiny hole near the front of the vulva called the urethra is used to pee. Behind the urethra is another, bigger hole called the vagina.

Some babies' bodies don't fit into either group. These babies are sometimes known as "intersex."

We all hear lots of ideas about how people should look, dress, and behave because they were born with a penis or a vulva. These are just that: ideas. Everyone gets to decide for themselves what they like.

"My favorite hobbies are baking cakes and playing soccer."

"I HATE the color pink."

"I like to be called 'they,' not 'he' or 'she.'"

But what does this have to do with growing up?

As you grow up, your body will start to change. These changes happen to get your body ready to make a baby when you are older, if you want to. This change is called puberty and it happens at different times for different people.

Puberty begins when your brain tells your ovaries or your testicles to start releasing hormones, which begin to make your body grow and change.

"Isn't the world AMAZING!"

For some children puberty can begin at around age eight, but for others it might happen at age 14 or older.

Although a hormone's main job is to tell your body to start to work in new ways, hormones can also make you feel very different too.

You might sometimes feel happier than you have ever felt, and at other times upset, angry, or frustrated, even if you don't quite understand why. These strong feelings are sometimes known as mood swings.

Testicles release a hormone called testosterone.

Penis

Testicles

Ovaries release a hormone called estrogen.

Womb

Vagina

"Isn't the world DEPRESSING!"

Not every grown-up can or will choose to use their body to make a baby. There are lots of different ways to be a grown-up.

When puberty starts, the first thing you will probably notice is that you start getting taller!

Sometimes you might see very thin white, red, or purple stretch marks where your body and skin has grown very fast. These will fade over time.

You will probably start to grow hair in places where you have never had any before, such as under your arms, and around your vulva or at the base of your penis.

The tiny hairs that cover your arms, legs, upper lip, and face may start to get a bit darker and thicker too.

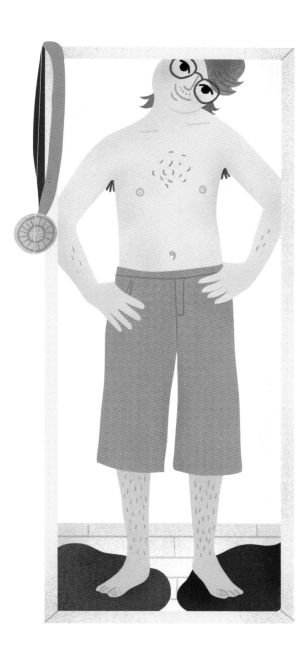

This is also the time when pimples might start to appear on your face, back, or chest. Some people hardly have any, and some people have lots. It's important not to pick them, or you could make them sore.

Puberty also makes you sweat more, which can make you start to smell. Washing regularly will help keep you feeling clean and smelling fresh.

Some people might also want to try using deodorant or antiperspirant. These are sticks, roll-ons, or gels worn under the armpits, to mask the smell of sweat or make you sweat less.

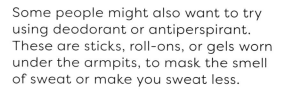

Along with looking after your hair and cleaning your teeth, learning how to care for your body properly is an important part of growing up.

By around the age of nine to twelve, many people born with a vulva will start to grow breasts.

Breasts and nipples come in all shapes, colors, and sizes. Every person's body is unique! At first, some people may feel small sore bumps behind their nipples, which get bigger and less sore over time. Nipples can also get larger and darker.

Sports bra

Wire bra

Bralette

Some people might find their breasts hurt when they run, exercise, or play sports. Wearing a bra can help them feel more comfortable, especially if they have larger breasts.

Many people born with a vulva will also find that their hips will start to get wider and their bottoms a bit bigger once puberty has started.

They might also start to notice marks in their underwear where their vagina has made a small amount of clear, yellow, or white liquid. This is a normal part of the vagina cleaning itself.

These changes happen at a different speed for everyone, and some people's bodies will change more than others.

During puberty, most people born with a vulva will start having periods. This is one of the ways their body starts to get ready to grow a baby one day.

Inside the body of a person with a vulva is usually a womb and two ovaries. A womb is where a baby is grown.

Ovaries make and store eggs. Eggs are needed to help grown-ups make a baby, if they want to. Each egg is about the size of a very sharp pencil point.

When puberty starts, hormones tell a person's ovaries to send an egg down a tube from one of their ovaries to their womb.

The womb starts to get ready for the egg, just in case this egg is going to turn into a baby, by growing a soft layer of cells with lots of blood in them for the egg to grow on.

If the egg does not turn into a baby, the womb gets rid of the blood, egg, and other cells.

These cells travel down and out of the vagina as drops of blood.

This is called a period.

For many people, periods will last for between three and eight days and will happen about once a month. Other people might have much longer or shorter gaps between periods. Most people stop having periods between the age of 45 and 55.

Periods affect different people in different ways, and everyone who has periods will find their own ways of dealing with them.

Reusable pad

Single-use pad

Some people stick pads inside their underwear to catch any blood . . .

Underwear

. . . and some people use specially lined period underwear to catch the blood instead.

Cup

Tampons

Other people use tampons or reusable rubber cups which are put inside the vagina.

Some people might find that their breasts become sore before they have a period. They might also have some up-and-down feelings or mood swings, because of the hormones that are traveling around their body.

Other people might notice their skin has a few more breakouts, just before or while they are having their period.

Periods can sometimes cause people to have a bit of a sore, uncomfortable feeling in their tummy, but most people can keep doing everything they would usually do.

If you have questions about your period or you want to speak to someone about what it's like having periods, talk to a grown-up you trust who will be able to help you.

Around the age of 12 to 14, many people born with a penis will be starting to get taller and more hairy.

"I use an electric shaver now and then."

"I like to keep my eyebrows looking neat."

As well as growing hair under their arms and around the base of their penis, people often start to grow hair on their faces, chests, and sometimes on their backs.

Beard and moustache hair might grow in patches at first. Some people are happy to let it grow, but others start using a razor to get rid of the hair. This takes a lot of practice and you might want to get a grown-up you trust to help you at first.

"I use a razor and shaving cream every day."

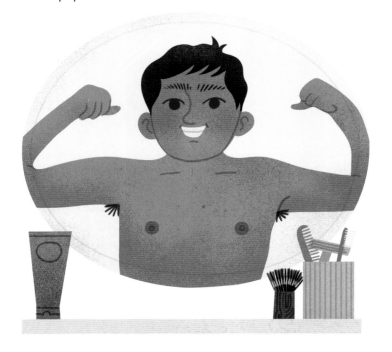

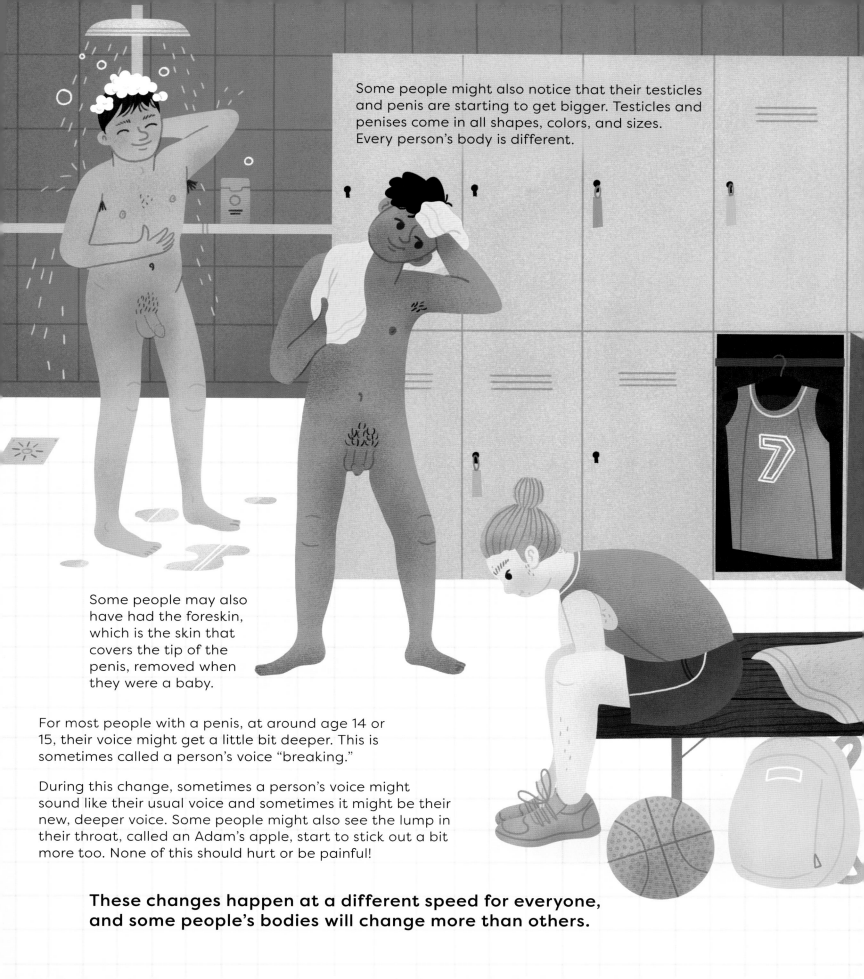

Some people might also notice that their testicles and penis are starting to get bigger. Testicles and penises come in all shapes, colors, and sizes. Every person's body is different.

Some people may also have had the foreskin, which is the skin that covers the tip of the penis, removed when they were a baby.

For most people with a penis, at around age 14 or 15, their voice might get a little bit deeper. This is sometimes called a person's voice "breaking."

During this change, sometimes a person's voice might sound like their usual voice and sometimes it might be their new, deeper voice. Some people might also see the lump in their throat, called an Adam's apple, start to stick out a bit more too. None of this should hurt or be painful!

These changes happen at a different speed for everyone, and some people's bodies will change more than others.

During puberty, most people born with a penis will start noticing that their penis becomes stiff, bigger, and lifts away from their body to point upward more often. This is called an erection.

Erections can happen without warning at any time of day or night.

Testicles are where sperm are made. Sperm are needed to help grown-ups make a baby, if they want to. They are teeny-tiny and have wiggly tails like tadpoles.

At night when a person is sleeping, they might have an erection that leads to some of the sperm from inside their testicles coming out of the tip of their penis, along with some sticky white liquid.

This is often called a "wet dream," but it doesn't mean that they have wet the bed.

A person can't stop themselves from having a wet dream any more than they can stop themselves from sneezing!

Wet dreams are a completely normal part of puberty. They usually stop by the time a person is a grown-up.

It's not just what you look like that changes when you go through puberty. The way you feel inside can change too.

When there are a lot of hormones traveling around your body, it is normal to have feelings that are bigger and more powerful than ever before.

Sometimes, you might have very strong feelings about some of your friends. You might think they are the best people in the world and want to spend every single moment with them. If they feel the same way, that can be great!

But if they don't feel the same way, that can make you feel sad and angry.

Or maybe you are a person who has been spending a lot of time with friends who really don't make you feel happy at all.

Sometimes your friends will like the same things as you, and sometimes you will be very different. Learning to respect each other's differences is an important part of growing up.

It is completely normal for your friendships to change as you get older, and for some friendships to get stronger while others come to an end.

Sometimes it is better to stop spending time with friends who don't make you feel happy or good about yourself and start again. And sometimes, as we grow up, we rediscover our old friends.

If you have any friends who are making you feel sad, worried, or are hurting you, talk to a grown-up you trust, who will be able to help.

Part of growing up is learning to understand boundaries, which means learning what feels OK and what doesn't feel OK for you and for people around you.

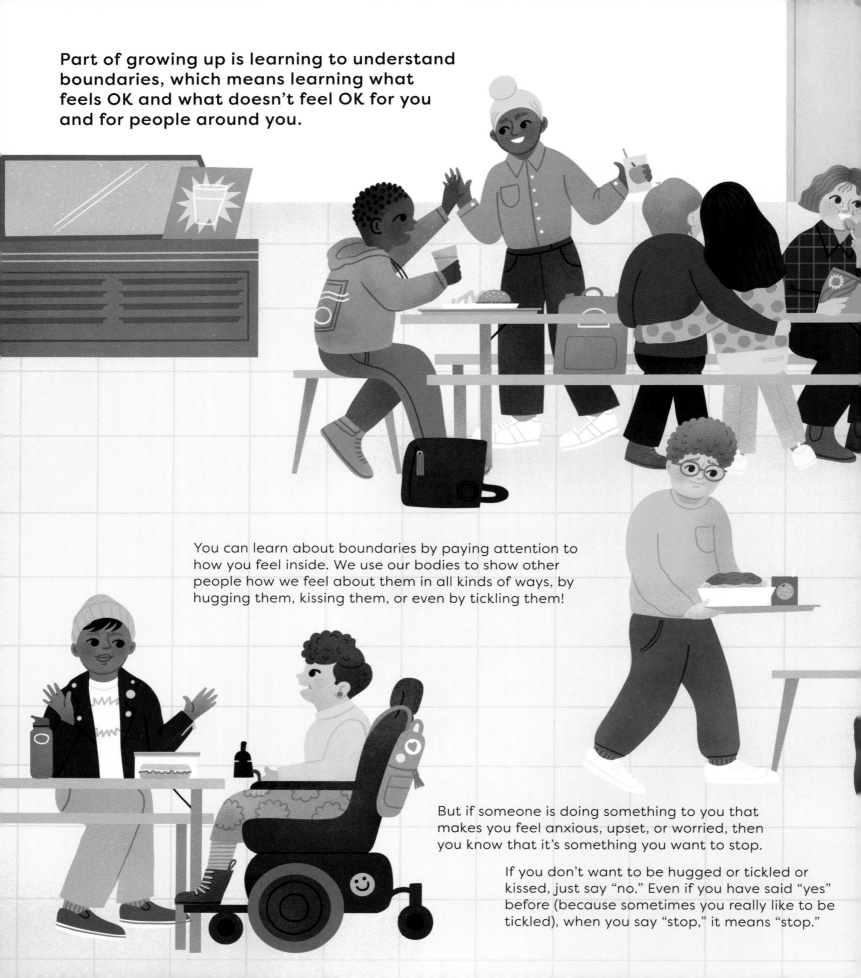

You can learn about boundaries by paying attention to how you feel inside. We use our bodies to show other people how we feel about them in all kinds of ways, by hugging them, kissing them, or even by tickling them!

But if someone is doing something to you that makes you feel anxious, upset, or worried, then you know that it's something you want to stop.

If you don't want to be hugged or tickled or kissed, just say "no." Even if you have said "yes" before (because sometimes you really like to be tickled), when you say "stop," it means "stop."

We also need to listen to other people when they tell us how they feel. "Stop" always means "stop" and "no" always means "no."

It's especially important to say "no" if someone asks you to show them a part of your body you don't want to show them, or asks to touch a part of your body that you don't want them to touch. If that person doesn't listen, tell a grown-up you trust right away.

Sometimes, you might feel like you need to behave a certain way to fit in with your friends.

It can be hard to be the person who says "no" but learning how to make up your own mind and behave the way you think is right is all part of becoming a grown-up. You're in charge of yourself!

Smartphones, tablets, and computers can be great. You can keep in touch with friends and family, watch videos online, and even play games. But to keep screen time fun, you need to be smart about how you use your device.

Sometimes, people you already know can behave differently online to the way they behave in real life. They might say things in messages that are mean or ask you to do things that make you feel anxious, upset, or worried.

You should always tell a grown-up you trust if someone has sent you unkind messages or is asking you to do something that makes you feel uncomfortable.

Sometimes, you might want to watch one thing online, but something else comes on instead. If you see anything that you don't like or don't understand, turn the device off and ask a grown-up you trust to help you find the right thing.

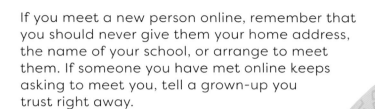

If you meet a new person online, remember that you should never give them your home address, the name of your school, or arrange to meet them. If someone you have met online keeps asking to meet you, tell a grown-up you trust right away.

Always remember to behave in the same way online as you would in real life. If you wouldn't say something to someone in real life, don't say it at all!

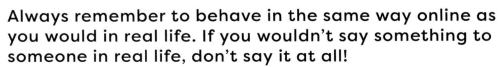

It might seem impossible now that one day you will be a grown-up, but puberty happens to everyone.

Your journey from being a child to becoming a grown-up will be as unique and special as you are!

What is a person's sex?

When a baby is born, a doctor or a midwife looks to see whether the baby has a penis or a vulva. Babies that have a penis are called boys (males). Babies that have a vulva are called girls (females). This is called their biological sex.

As babies get older and become children, they start to understand more about themselves and who they are. Lots of people will feel like the sex they were given when they were born is the right one for them.

Some people might feel that they weren't given the right sex when they were born: for example, they might have been called a girl when they were born, but actually they know they are a boy; or they might have been called a boy when they were born, but they know they are a girl.

Some people will feel like they're not a boy or a girl at all, or their feelings may change from day to day. Feeling like a boy or a girl, or neither, or both, is called a person's gender identity. Everyone has a gender identity. Some people will know what their gender identity is when they are very young and some people might only feel sure when they are a teenager or a grown-up.

Why is online safety so important?

Whenever you post something online, it is there forever. This is called a person's digital footprint, and your digital footprint will grow with you as you grow up.

If you send a digital photo of yourself to another person, once that person has that picture you cannot control who they show it to or whether they put it online.

It is especially important not to take or send photos of private parts of your body to send to someone else. If anyone asks you to do this, tell a grown-up you trust right away.

Online and text message bullying is also known as cyberbullying. It is very serious, especially if hurtful comments are being made about a person because of who they are, for example: about the color of their skin, the fact that they need special equipment to help them hear or move around, their religion, or the fact that they have two moms, or two dads, or live with their grandma. If you experience cyberbullying, you must tell a grown-up you trust as soon as possible.

Finding Help

When you start going through puberty, you might find the changes confusing or upsetting, especially if your body is changing in ways that make you feel uncomfortable. The most important thing you can do is to talk to a trusted adult. This might be a parent, grandparent, foster parent, caregiver, teacher, doctor, school nurse, or counselor.

If you still have questions or would like to speak to someone in confidence, there are organizations that you can contact for free online, by phone, or by text for help and advice.

AMAZE
www.amaze.org

The Trevor Project
www.thetrevorproject.org

Glossary

Biological sex
The biological sex of a baby is usually decided by whether they have a **vulva** or a **penis** when they are born.

Breasts
Breasts grow on your chest. When a person gives birth to a baby, breasts produce milk that can be used to feed the baby.

Cyberbullying
Bullying that takes place online or via text message or chat group.

Digital footprint
Things you have put online over your lifetime such as comments and pictures.

Eggs
Eggs are made inside a person's **ovaries** and are needed to help make a baby.

Erection
When a **penis** becomes stiff and stands up.

Female
This word is used to describe a baby's **biological sex** if they are born with a vulva.

Gender identity
The feeling of being a boy or a girl, or neither, or both.

Hormone
A chemical message made by your body that tells other parts of your body to change or start to work in new ways.

Intersex
This word is sometimes used to describe a baby's **biological sex** if their body has parts that are like a **penis** and parts that are like a **vulva**.

Male
This word is used to describe a baby's **biological sex** if they are born with a **penis**.

Ovaries
These are where **eggs** are made and stored.

Penis
The penis sits outside of the body in front of the **testicles**.

Period
Blood and cells that travel down from the **womb** and out of the **vagina**.

Puberty
The time in a person's life when their body changes from a child's body to a grown-up body.

Sperm
Sperm are made inside a person's **testicles** and are needed to help make a baby.

Testicles
The testicles sit outside of the body behind the **penis**. **Sperm** are made here.

Urethra
This tube carries pee out of the body through a hole in the tip of the **penis** or at the front of the **vulva**.

Vagina
The **vagina** is a tube which leads from the **womb** to the **vulva**.

Vulva
The vulva is on the outside of the body and is made of many parts. At the front is a tiny hole leading to a tube called the **urethra** which is used to pee. Behind the urethra is a bigger hole leading to a tube called the **vagina**.

Wet dream
An erection when someone is sleeping that leads to **sperm** from a person's **testicles** coming out of the tip of their **penis**, along with some sticky white liquid.

Womb
This is the place where **periods** come from and where a baby can be grown.